ALL ABOUT
Coding Variables

BY JAMES BOW

Published by The Child's World®
1980 Lookout Drive • Mankato, MN 56003-1705
800-599-READ • www.childsworld.com

Photographs ©: Lorelyn Medina/Shutterstock Images,
cover (top girl), cover (coins), cover (bottom girl), 1
(top girl), 1 (coins), 1 (bottom girl), 24; Viki Vector/
Shutterstock Images, cover (top piggy bank), 1
(top piggy bank), 15; Shutterstock Images, cover
(bottom piggy bank), 1 (bottom piggy bank), 6, 9,
17, 18; People Image Studio/Shutterstock Images,
5; Carla Edwards/Shutterstock Images, 13

ISBN 9781503832022
LCCN 2018962837

Printed in the United States of America
PA02418

ABOUT THE AUTHOR

James Bow is the author of more than 60 nonfiction books for children. He is a graduate of the University of Waterloo in Ontario, Canada, and is a freelance writer, editor, and web designer. He currently lives outside Toronto with his wife and two daughters.

TABLE OF CONTENTS

CHAPTER 1

What Are Variables?

Sarah is saving her money to buy a new bicycle. Every time she earns money, she puts it into her piggy bank. When Sarah adds money to her piggy bank, she writes down what she added.

That's a lot of work. A computer could make this easier by remembering how much money is in the piggy bank. It could also keep track of the money Sarah adds to her piggy bank. A computer would do this using **code**. Code tells a computer what to do. The parts of code that tell a computer to remember a number, word, or anything else are called **variables**.

Variables in code could help Sarah know how much money is in her piggy bank.

Variables help computers remember values by taking their place in the code.

```
sidebar.js
  ∨ signin
      signin.js
  ∨ models
      account.js
      agency.js
      collection.js
      photo.js
      sale.js
      settings.js
      stats.js
  ∨ utils
      database.js
      helpers.js
      prototypes.js
  ∨ views
    > dashboard
    ∨ misc
        chart.mustache
```

```
◄ ►  signin.js   ○   sidebar.js        best_selling.js      worker.js       side
1    define([
2        'can',
3        'models/account',
4        'controls/dashboard/dashboard',
5        'controls/misc/titlebar',
6        'toastr',
7        'moment',
8        'utils/helpers'
9    ], function(can, Account, Dashboard, Titlebar, Toastr,
10       return can.Control.extend({
11           defaults: new can.Map({
12               success: null,
13               error: null,
14               username: null,
15               passowrd: null
16           }
17       },{
18           init: function() {
19               var self = this;
20               this.element.html(can.view('//app/src/views/
21               this.element.parent().addClass('login-screen
22
23               App.db.getSettings().then(function(settings)
24                   App.attr('settings', settings);
25                   self.element.find('#login-remember').pro
26
27                   App.db.getLoggedAccount().then(function(
28                       if(account) {
29                           self.options.attr('username', ac
30                           self.options.attr('password', ac
31
32                           if(account.attr('username') && a
33                               self.signin(account.attr('us
34                           }
35                       }
36                   });
37               });
38
39               new Titlebar('#titlebar');
40           },
```

Variables help computers remember different **values**. Variables take the place of those values in the code. Any time a computer needs to remember a value, a variable will store that value in the computer's memory. Sometimes values change. When a value changes, a variable tells the code the new value. This keeps the computer code running smoothly.

CHAPTER 2

Different Types of Variables

Variables store values, but not all values are the same. Values such as "1," "Mr. Stevens," and "$5" could all be stored using different types of variables. **Integer** variables help store numbers. String variables help store words and letters. A third type of variable is a **Boolean** variable. This variable remembers whether a value is true or false. Boolean values answer yes or no questions. If the answer is yes, the value is true. If the answer is no, the value is false.

Letters are values that string variables remember.

Each type of variable can only be used with values of the same type. Integer variables can only be used with numbers. For example, the number 20 cannot be multiplied by the word *dog*. That doesn't make sense. String variables can only be used with words and letters. A number can be used in a string variable, but it would be treated like a letter or a word.

STRING VARIABLES

The code below makes a computer print first and last names together. This code uses string variables. In one set of code, "John" is the value of the variable called first_name. The value of last_name is " Smith." There is a space before *Smith*. So the computer prints "John Smith." In the other set of code, the values are changed from words to numbers. The code treats the new values like words because they are in string variables. This code prints "23" instead of "5."

```
John + Smith

String first_name = "John"
String last_name = " Smith"
print (first_name + last_name)
                    --John Smith
```

```
2 + 3

String first_name = "2"
String last_name = "3"
print (first_name + last_name)
                    --23
```

CHAPTER 3

Declaring Variables

Coders must say what types of variables they are using. They say whether the variables are integer, string, or Boolean variables. Then, they have to name their variables.

Each variable needs to have a different name. The name is how the computer remembers the variable and its value. The name is like an address in a city. Just as two buildings cannot be at the same address, two variables cannot be stored in the same part of a computer's memory.

After naming their variables, coders can give them starting values. Writing the name, type, and value of a variable is called declaring a variable.

2·2·2

Variables need different names just as buildings need different addresses.

Suppose a store owner wants to use a variable to keep track of how many boxes of cereal the store has. She first writes what type of variable she is using and gives it a name. She then gives the variable a starting value. Right now, the store has 99 boxes of cereal. So "99" is the starting value of the variable. Then she has the code subtract one box of cereal from the starting value each time a box is sold. The variable remembers the new total. Now the computer will always know how many boxes of cereal the store has.

```
int Cereal = 99;
Cereal = Cereal - 1
```

In the example above, the *int* shows that the variable is an integer, which is a type of number. The variable's name is Cereal, and "99" is the starting value.

CHAPTER 4

Ways to Use Variables

There are many uses for variables. Variables can keep track of goods for sale in a store. When a value goes below a certain number, a set of code can tell a computer that it is time to order more of those products.

A variable can also count the number of times something happens. If a computer needs to print something ten times, a program runs a set of code repeatedly in a **loop**. The variable counts the number of times the computer goes through the loop. Once it has gone through the loop ten times, the computer stops printing.

Variables can remember how much of a certain product a store has.

Variables can help track how far someone has gone.

Variables can also help with math. For example, Simon wants to measure how far he walks in a month, but he can only write down how far he walks each day. A variable remembers how far Simon walked on day one. When Simon adds how much he walked on day two, the variable adds the two numbers together and remembers the result. This continues until the end of the month.

These are only some of the ways variables are used in computer code. Variables turn computer code into programs that can handle hard tasks. Without variables, computers would not be able to do as much as they do now.

Q: Which of the following is not a type of variable?

a. string

b. loop

c. integer

d. Boolean

A: b. loop

Q: Why does each variable need its own name?

A: A variable's name is like an address to a part of a computer's memory. There cannot be more than one variable at the same address.

Q: What is part of declaring a variable?

    a. giving the variable a name

    b. stating what type of variable it is

    c. giving the variable a starting value

    d. all of the above

A: d. all of the above

Q: What is a Boolean variable?

A: A Boolean variable remembers values that are true or false.

GLOSSARY

Boolean (BOO-lee-un) Something is Boolean if it can only be true or false. The Boolean variable remembers values that are true or false.

code (KOHD) Code is a list of instructions that computers follow to do things. The code told the computer to keep track of the money.

coders (KOHD-urz) Coders are people who write code. Coders use variables in their code.

integer (IN-tuh-jur) An integer is a whole number. The integer 3 can be remembered by a variable.

loop (LOOP) A loop is a type of code that tells a computer to repeat an action. The loop told the computer to print something ten times.

values (VAL-yooz) Values are words, letters, and numbers that computer code uses. Variables remember values.

variables (VAYR-ee-uh-buhlz) Variables are a type of code that helps a computer remember things. Variables can keep track of how much money is in a bank.

IN THE LIBRARY

Miller, Derek L. *Information and Action: Using Variables*.
New York, NY: Cavendish Square Publishing, 2018.

Wood, Kevin. *Get Coding with Data*.
New York, NY: Rosen Publishing, 2018.

Woodcock, Jon. *DK Workbooks: Computer Coding*.
New York, NY: DK Publishing, 2014.

ON THE WEB

Visit our website for links about coding:
childsworld.com/links

Note to Parents, Teachers, and Librarians: We routinely verify our
Web links to make sure they are safe and active sites.
So encourage your readers to check them out!

INDEX